Photo: Andy Rasheedeyefood.

Playwright Finegan Kruckemeyer has written over 57 plays. His work has been performed both nationally and internationally, in 50 Australian/international festivals; five IPAYH American showcases; five UK tours; and at venues including the Sydney Opera House, New York's New Victory Theater, Edinburgh's Imaginate Festival, Dublin's Abbey Theatre, Shanghai's Malan Flower Theatre and DC's Kennedy Center.

He was the inaugural recipient of the 2001 Sidney Myer Creative Fellowship. Other awards include the 2012 Helpmann Award for Children's Theatre, 2010 Rodney Seaborn Award, 2009 AWGIE Award (Best Australian Children's Play), 2008 Oscart (Best Children's Playwright), 2007 Oscart (Best Playwright), 2006 Jill Blewett Award, and 2002 Colin Thiele Scholarship.

In 2013, Finegan is the Keynote Speaker at the One Theatre World North American TYA Conference. He has also spoken at events in Argentina, Australia, Austria, Denmark, England, Indonesia, Scotland, Sweden and the US. He has also had essays published.

Finegan lives in Tasmania with his wife, Essie.

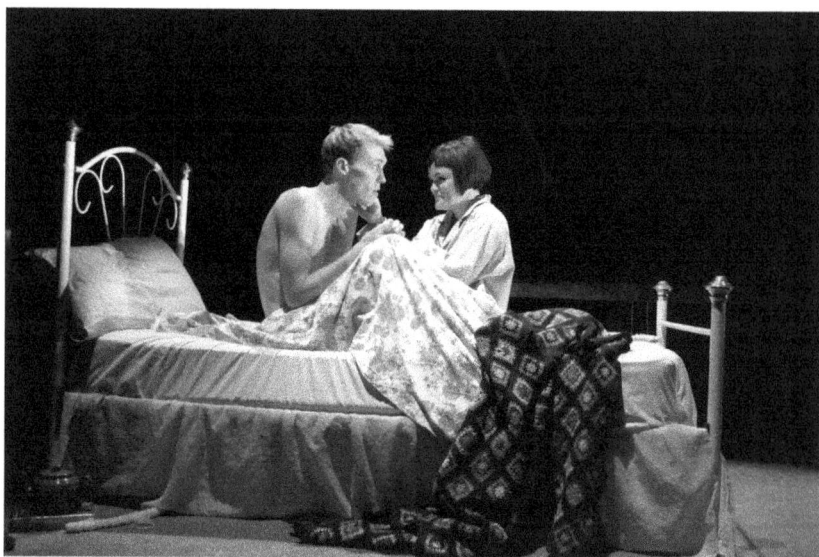

Christiaan Westerveld as Caleb and Laura Pegrum as Sylvia in the 2012
Jute Theatre production in Cairns. (Photo: Romy Photography)

AT SEA,

STARING UP

FINEGAN KRUCKEMEYER

CURRENCY PLAYS

First published in 2013
by Currency Press Pty Ltd,
PO Box 2287, Strawberry Hills, NSW, 2012, Australia
enquiries@currency.com.au
www.currency.com.au

NATIONAL LIBRARY OF AUSTRALIA CIP DATA

Author: Kruckemeyer, Finegan.
Title: At sea, staring up / Finegan Kruckemeyer.
ISBN: 9780868199641 (pbk.)
Dewey Number: A822.4

Typeset by Claire Grady for Currency Press.
Front cover shows: (from left) Brett Walsh as Noah, Ella Watson-Russell as Elise, Natalie Taylor as Emma, Christiaan Westerveld as Caleb and Laura Pegrum as Sylvia in the 2012 Jute Theatre production in Cairns. (Photo: Romy Photography)
Cover design by Katy Wall for Currency Press.

At Sea, Staring Up was created with assistance from the Commonwealth Government through the Australia Council, its arts funding and advisory body.

Contents

Currency Press acknowledges the Traditional Owners of the Country on which we live and work. We pay our respects to all Aboriginal and Torres Strait Islander Elders, past and present.

Collaborating to create theatrical magic

Suellen Maunder

Many of the projects that I work on begin with the fusion of seemingly unrelated events, ideas, people and dreams. This was indeed the case with *At Sea, Staring Up*.

I am a founding member and artistic director of JUTE, a regional theatre company that over the last twenty years has developed and produced writers from regional and geographically isolated areas. I first met Finegan, or Fin, in 2007 when he took part in JUTE's national emerging playwright program, devised to bring a number of young and emerging writers together from the far flung reaches of Australia, including regional Queensland, Northern Territory, Western Australia and Tasmania. This group went on to collaborate on a new work entitled *Dancing Back Home*, which was subsequently co-produced in 2010 by JUTE Theatre Company and Mudlark Theatre in Launceston.

Also in 2010, five very interesting emerging and early career performers, ranging in age from twenty to twenty-eight, auditioned for JUTE. It seemed to be too good an opportunity to waste, such good potential all in the one place at the one time, so I set about creating a project that would be about and for them. I'd been looking for a vehicle to celebrate JUTE's twentieth anniversary in 2012, and thought these young actors would be perfect.

So I had the actors, next I needed the writer, and Fin was the obvious choice. Since 2007, when we first collaborated with Fin, his career had taken off. His generosity, his leadership qualities and his genuine connection with people led me to believe that he would engage well with the performers; but more than anything, it was the innocence and magical tenderness of Fin's work that resonated with me and convinced me that he was perfect for the job.

The final pieces of the puzzle were Peter Matheson, JUTE's dramaturg, and Essie Kruckemeyer, Fin's wife, whose role was emerging dramaturg. I was reluctant for Fin to begin too much work before meeting the actors: they were to be a key inspiration and integral to the script development. In January 2011 we were finally all in the same room. Our early conversations focused on form rather than the specifics of the story.

The first production of *At Sea, Staring Up* would be in 2012—the year of the Dragon. There was something in the strength and power of the dragon image; the large sweep of wings, the gothic fairytale nature of this mythical creature that opened the way for epic storytelling. Water was another recurring theme in those first days, but it wasn't until later in the process that the four seasons emerged as the key to unlock the journey of the characters. Being based in Cairns, I was eager to transport our audience out of our sometimes overwhelming tropical environment and take them somewhere very different while not losing the connection to this place, and so the idea for a work that jumped continents developed.

The first day was spent allowing the performers to bring their inspirations to the room; listening to their stories, the rhythm of their speech, the natural style of their storytelling, and in observing their physicality. We set up some improvisations around character traits and began to play with how these characters might interact. Music was an important inspiration at this point and confirmed for me that music and soundscape would be key elements of the final production.

Throughout this improvisational play, Fin gathered not only character ideas but a sense of the rhythm of the dialogue, as well as the elements of the piece. The stories and characters that evolved into *At Sea, Staring Up* were not generated by the actors, but were rather inspired by them; grown from listening and observing them in the rehearsal space.

It wasn't long before short monologues and pieces of dialogue began flowing from Fin. We took these pieces, hot off the press, as it were, and started playing with them on the floor, giving the actors some provocations, circumstances, times and places and allowing them to make connections between these elements and the other characters. I say 'we', because sometimes Fin would set up an improvisation that would feed directly into where his ideas were taking him with the work. The room was very fluid, with input from the dramaturges, as well as the actors, Fin and myself. We filmed these early improvisations, and looking back on them it's easy to see where ideas sparked and took hold, even if they were subconscious at the time. An improvisation from an actor talking about how he liked to visit his favourite aunty in Leeds, who gave him a little plastic toy, a diver in a wet suit, inspired moments in two characters' journeys. Another actor, talking about what the four seasons meant to the character he was inhabiting, talked about how winter allowed him to dream about being isolated; adrift in the ocean.

Taking the text to the floor at this point meant that it was already informed by the improvisations around music, physical elements, the sense of ensemble that was being built and the stories that had been created around the emerging characters. Short scenes were played with, ditched, cut to pieces, reformatted, then played with again. Still, these were only starting points for character development. As these five characters emerged, we continued to swap actors around so that there was no sense of ownership of a particular role, enabling the characters to continue to be informed by all of the actors.

At the culmination of the creative development we presented our findings to an invited group of industry peers. Many of the short pieces presented on that final day still exist in the play and these formed the bones from which Fin built the remainder of the work. It was clear by the end of the creative development that something special was emerging, and JUTE committed to its production for our anniversary.

The process was very open and organic, yet consistently rigorous in its drive towards the creation of a beautiful piece of writing. There was something very special about the sense of collective ownership of the work that was felt by the actors, which continued into the rehearsal process and through the production in 2012. We are all very proud of the work that was achieved. The following pages present the result of Fin's ability to take this collaboration and from it, create theatrical magic.

Suellen Maunder
February 2013

Suellen Maunder is a founding member, Artistic Director and CEO of JUTE Theatre Company. She is also an actor and director.

Natalie Taylor as Emma in the 2012 Jute Theatre production in Cairns. (Photo: Romy Photography)

At Sea, Staring Up was first produced by JUTE Theatre Company at JUTE Theatre, Cairns, on 9 March 2012, with the following cast:

SYLVIA WIST	Laura Pegrum
EMMA THE GREEK	Natalie Taylor
NOAH KEARNEY	Brett Walsh
ELISE DABELSTEIN	Ella Watson-Russell
CALEB PROSSER	Christiaan Westerveld

All other roles were played by the company.

Director, Suellen Maunder
Designer, Luke Ede
Lighting Designer, Jason Glenwright
Sound Designer, Quincy Grant
Dramaturg, Peter Matheson
Assistant Dramaturg, Esther Kruckemeyer

CHARACTERS

SYLVIA WIST, Australian
NOAH KEARNEY, English
ELISE DABELSTEIN, German
EMMA THE GREEK, Icelandic
CALEB PROSSER, Australian
PADDY, Emma's brother
ULLI, Emma's brother
PAPA, Emma's father
A MAN
MATTHIAS

A NOTE ON THE TEXT

When a backslash (/) appears within the dialogue, it indicates overlapping dialogue.

ACKNOWLEDGEMENTS

As well as those Juters who so generously watched and responded, Finegan would like to acknowledge that this play was written on an island and that during those most formative months, Hobartian friends offered invaluable feedback. Thanks to Guy, Matt, Mel, Jemma and Sally for providing first voices, and to Denise, Frank and Magdalena for offering your ears. And this writer believes there is no gift so great as a dramaturgical wife, who can see potential in some first words, and help wave goodbye to others—thank you Essie.

PROLOGUE

ELISE: In Serbia, the women carry glasses of whisky to the tables where the men sit. And they peer at their husband's cards, and work out the coins on the table, and work out if they'll be bought a green dress or not.

CALEB: In Canada, there is a house in the woods where every man of one family for fourteen generations has gone to die.

EMMA: In Korea, the old women tell tales of when they were girls, and when dragons still roamed the earth. They weren't bad dragons then, and for the gift of a cow, they would fly over the sea and tell to the fishers where the tuna swam.

NOAH: In the south of Ireland, seven wild horses found their way to the top of an overgrown hill, and slept in the ruins of a castle.

    SYLVIA *stands at a bottling plant.*

SYLVIA: On March fourteenth 2001 in Wendeburg, Germany, there is a dance in the town square and a woman called Elise twirls her husband—like the roles are reversed—and laughs and laughs.

    It is depicted.

On March fourteenth 2001 in Bristol, England, a young man skims a stone so successfully, he can no longer see the point at which it disappears.

    It is depicted.

On March fourteenth 2001 during a Contiki Tour in Vanuatu, a man is hit in the face for offering to buy a woman a drink.

    It is depicted.

CALEB: Fuck!

SYLVIA: On March fourteenth 2001 at latitude fourteen, longitude twenty-two, a large ship is split in two by forces unknown, with all hands lost.

    EMMA *stares shocked at corpses floating around her and tentatively pokes one. Silence.*

EMMA: Hello, dead man… Why are there so many of you dead?

SYLVIA: On March fourteenth 2001 in Innisfail, Australia, a girl called Sylvia Wist is on her way to school when she is pulled tumbling through the folds of time and dropped unceremoniously in a small hallway in Greece. There, through an open door, she spends long minutes watching a woman bake a cake and a baby cry, until the vice-like grip of chance and improbability lifts her once again and returns her to the Australian footpath. She collapses into the gutter and whispers: 'What is wrong with me?'

And when the passing bus driver stops to check on her ten minutes later, she still lacks an answer.

Autumn

SCENE ONE

SYLVIA: Ten years later, in 2011, it's Autumn in Bristol, England, and a tall man rises unsteadily from his seat, and taps a small glass with a dessert spoon.

NOAH: Okay, speeches! Dear family and frie— oh, I'm a bit drunk.

> *Laughter.*

Shut up—okay! Dearly beloved, we are gathered here today to— oh no, done that bit. Ha!— No…

Seriously…

Dear… dear people that Sophia and I love so much. You're here today because… you're very important in our lives. My family and friends here in England, and Sophia's amazing relatives who've travelled across from Italy—which shows who loves us the most! Ha.

Seriously… My love for you all… for sharing this day with us, and sharing our lives with us, pales only in comparison to… to my love for the lady sitting there.

> *The crowd oohs.* NOAH *silences them.*

Sophia Ubaldi, you are… I don't know… everything I dreamed I'd one day find. And to be honest… I never thought I'd actually find it.

I thought it was… There are no words for it. I've found my love. And suddenly everything, absolutely everything, feels okay— 'cause of you…

My fucking gorgeous Italian wife!

> *Cheering.*

Ha! Cheers everyone! Cheers!

SCENE TWO

SYLVIA, *falling asleep, bottles at the conveyor belt.* CALEB, *asleep, flounders at sea.*

SYLVIA: In Australia, a man succumbs to a nightmare ocean and lets himself be swallowed up by the waves. The frustrating thing for the man, however, is he forgets to drown. And the man says:

Both jerk back to consciousness.

CALEB: Help! Help! Help me!

SYLVIA: But the waves are large and eat his words.

And that morning, the girl Sylvia Wist finishes a night shift and goes to bed. And that morning, the boy Caleb Prosser finishes a nightmare and rises. And she falls into sleep. He falls into his clothes. She loses her conscious state. He loses his spot in the coffee line 'cause of a phone call.

CALEB: Oh come on.

SYLVIA: She enters her dream state. He enters the lift at work. And she dreams now…

That she's standing in a small space, and holding a man she's never met. She is dreaming that she loves him. She is dreaming that she kisses his neck. She is dreaming he holds her breasts. She is dreaming that they are whispering:

CALEB: Don't let me go.

SYLVIA: But I'm not normal.

CALEB: I know you're not.

SYLVIA: No, *really* not normal.

CALEB: I know.

SYLVIA: And Sylvia Wist wakes from the dream… with her sheets soaked and the bedside lamp flickering.

And Caleb Prosser wakes from the dream still standing in the lift. But now he realises that Toby from Accounts stands beside him, looking shocked. And he realises also, that he has come.

And he realises he is fired.

SCENE THREE

EMMA: In the two weeks that me and my father and my two brothers are lost at sea, we floated a great distance. At one time on the tenth day, a large wave smashed a hole in the side and we had to take turns sitting on that bench and blocking it with our backs, and with our bottoms. I felt scared whenever it was my turn—my bottom was like bait I thought, for something in the sea. I did not wish my bottom to be eaten.

They call me Emma the Greek, but I am not Greek. I am olive-skinned though, and in Iceland this is odd enough for a nickname.

My mama was a slut and had me with a travelling sailor... says my father. He does not say if the sailor was Greek—he does not even know if this is true—but since forever Emma the Greek is my name.

I cannot ask my mama the truth, because the sea carries no messages to the ones who lie at the bottom of it. Or even if the sea does do this, it does not bring back to the surface the replies.

In the two weeks, we shared a little food that we saved from the trawler before it went down. We throw tin cans into the lifeboat quickly and my brother said:

PADDY: Not those ones Emma the Greek.

EMMA: And Papa said:

PAPA: Don't talk bullshit, Paddy. Food is food. Hurry up or I leave you here.

EMMA: Papa is unforgiving and a taskmaster, we say. But he saved us all from my mama's ocean and it is for this I have no problem with him. Thank you Papa.

On the twelfth day, my oldest brother Ulli said:

ULLI: One of us will not survive.

EMMA: And this was the biggest surprise, as Ulli has not said a one word for nine years. The doctor said he had a black hole grow in his brain one day, like exist in outer space, and the black hole sucked up all the words he had ever learnt in the twenty-two years before this, and then he has no more words. But I thought another thing—I thought was Ulli waiting for the right words.

On the last day, Papa says this is the coldest night coming and snow sat on the water around us, and we did not have to fear about the hole in the boat because the ice formed across it and blocked it—amazing. But Papa says:

PAPA: This is the coldest night, boys and girl. And Emma the Greek does not stop shivering.

EMMA: I am okay Papa.

PAPA: You shut up now Emma the Greek. Boys, you take your jackets off. I take my jacket off too—we give them to the girl.

PADDY: No Papa!

EMMA: Says Paddy. And Ulli, he say nothing. But they all take their jackets off and lay them on me, and I am too tired to argue, and I feel for the first time in days, warm. 'Why do they not make a normal jacket that is three jacket's thick', I think. 'This is a great invention.'

And then I go to sleep, and as my eyes are closing, I see Papa and Paddy and Ulli in their t-shirts, and they are sitting together at the end of the boat, huddled together, and Papa is rubbing both their shoulders like a great big bear. He is a very good father.

And later I wake up when we hit the land, and I smile at Papa and Ulli and Paddy. And two of them look at me. But Paddy has blue skin and a look that is not for us anymore, but for Mama now. He can talk to Mama now, I understand this straight away. And so before we tie the boat and step ashore, we give him to the sea.

Goodbye, Paddy Blue Skin.

SCENE FOUR

ELISE: He and I lie on the leaves together—near the edge of the water, beside the tree line, and we watch the dragons fly overhead. A great blanket of them passing in perfect formation—dipping in time with the eddying of the breeze, catching troughs and gusts of brave, cold wind, their bellies scaly reflections of the earth below.

My husband walks in the forest somewhere far behind us, showing my son the burrows where animals sleep, or carrying him on his shoulders so he can brush his small hand against the leaves of the heavy, silent trees.

The man stretches out his hand across the grass and reaches my thigh. He strokes the seam of my jeans—my ugly, faded jeans—just beside my knee, beside the indent. And not being religious, I pray that he will never stop, that my husband will lose his way in the woods, that my son will grow into a man without me, that the sun will stay right where it is, that time will stay right where it is.

The man returns his hand to beside him, to a safe distance, and above our heads the dragons dive and stare into our eyes as they come soaring—their sharp mouths wide—soaring down, down, down.

SCENE FIVE

CALEB: My name is Caleb Prosser and—
ALL: Hi Caleb.
CALEB: Oh. Right—hi. Um, where was I? I'm Caleb, and I… find it very hard to meet people.
> I'll stop there—I'm lying already. I find it very easy to meet people. I work in… a business that (I won't name it, if that's alright. Yep? Cool). And… anyway, my job *is* actually meeting people. Ha. I sit at a phone and I talk to people about their current share choices and portfolios, and what… financial investment they do currently make, and what investment they might be willing to make. And then if that potential investment is green-lighted by my computer then I… talk to my team— they're not my team. I talk to a team who are on a floor quite far above me. And… they give that person a call.
>
> So essentially I ring people who might be of interest. And if they *are* of interest… then they talk… to someone else.
>
> *Pause.*

MAN: And if they're not?
CALEB: Sorry?
MAN: If they're not of interest—who do they talk to then? Is that you?
CALEB: No—no-one. I thank them and… call the next person.
> Well, sorry, I don't actually. That's not true. I think maybe I don't do that job anymore. I'm not sure yet. Maybe I lost it yesterday.
MAN: Oh… But you don't know?
CALEB: It's… The circumstances were a bit… strange. I think they're working out what to do at the moment— Maybe they have—I should… is my phone on? Can we have phon— No. Cool. That's fair enough.
> *Pause.*

MAN: So, is there anything else you want to tell the group, Caleb? Anything at all is fine here.
CALEB: Oh right yeah, okay. Um… anything else… I have some hobbies.
MAN: Excellent. What are they?

CALEB: Heaps of them—ha. I am a member of about... forty-five associations.

MAN: Wow.

CALEB: I'm sorry?

MAN: Just... wow. That's impressive.

CALEB: Yeah. Um... right. Yeah, I love them. I'm an archer—I do archery. And er... water polo—I do that. I have recently become a member of the Afghani Kite-Fighting Society.

MAN: Oh. Are you from Afghanistan?

CALEB: No. I do, an evening Mahjong class. I'm an accredited basket weaver. I shoot.

MAN: Guns?

CALEB: Targets. I've tried gymnastic— oh right, sorry—shoot guns, yes. It's a gun club. I am learning some languages... I'm not good at them it seems, but... you know... trying them.

MAN: Well, this sounds really fantastic, Caleb. Sounds like some great networks of people out there that you're... you know, interacting with— with the... guns and kites and stuff. The gymnastics. It's wonderful.

CALEB: Mm. Yeah, thanks. Thanks—I've really made the effort, absolutely. But... I don't know. Lately I've been thinking, like...

Maybe a problem today is that people try to be wonderful at too much—maybe more than... than they can achieve. And actually some people (me, I'm basically talking about) they aren't actually good... at anything.

Like, they *do* lots. But they can't really *do*... anything.

Pause.

MAN: I'm sure there's some things you're good at.

CALEB: I think you'd be surprised.

MAN: Well... That's the point of Friends Helping Friends! We're here to support each other. So what we'll do is partner you up with someone who's been here a while and then next week—

CALEB: I won't be here next week.

MAN: Oh, okay. Well the week after then—

CALEB: No.

MAN: I'm sorry?

CALEB: I won't be here. I'm going away. In six days I go overseas. To my auntie's. In Bristol—for a while.

MAN: What? But... this, this is a group for... isolated people to form friendships, to build long-term friendships with each other. Didn't you know that, Caleb?

CALEB: Yes.

MAN: So... Sorry, why are you starting just before you leave?

CALEB: I'm... ah, good question. I don't know really. I saw the sign at my swing-dancing class and... I was free tonight. I was meant to be seeing a John Wayne movie, but I got the week wrong. Well, not the week as such, but... the cinema where it's playing this week is different to the one I thought. So I went to that one, the one I thought, but there was *My Fair Lady* on instead. And I don't really like musicals. But... well, I remembered this place was close by and I thought it was a, a nice coincidence with the dates. So... yeah, I came along. And then that guy... sorry is it Nick? Yeah, Nick—he talked about his son and... you know, he did all the, crying and stuff. And I... I wanted to leave earlier but—no offense, Nick—he just... was talking for so long... and crying, as well. Like, for a very long time...

Yeah.

Silence.

MAN: Caleb... Friends Helping Friends is a group designed for people to help each other. It's not about... dropping in when the movie you want to see isn't on.

CALEB: Oh right. Yeah, that makes sense.

Beat.

MAN: Could you please leave, Mr Prosser—

CALEB: Sure, yeah. Bye. Bye. Sorry about your son, Nick, and... you know, dying and stuff... Okay, yeah.

He exits. Silence. He returns.

CALEB: Sorry, I forgot my jacke— oh no. No it's in the car, that's right. Okay then.

Bye.

He exits.

SCENE SIX

SYLVIA *works at the conveyor belt.*

SYLVIA: I have two songs that were written about me—most people would feel lucky having one, but I've got two. The first one, which I got at the orphanage a long time ago, goes:
> *Sylvia Wist will never be kissed.*
> *And if she drowns, she won't be missed.*

That one was by Alison Lam and all the girls who sat with her at break, but mostly her, and they sang it while they were skipping. And the only time they let me skip with them, was if I agreed to sing it too.

Then in Year Nine, a boy called Sean Tiernan saw me do one of my *impossibilities* at the dam wall outside town. Because I was reading that salmon can only lay their eggs in one place upstream, in exactly the same place where they were born, and where their parents were born, and all the ones before them. So they swim against a river when they're pregnant, to get back to it. And if they have to, they swim up waterfalls.

And I was seeing if that was possible, not just for salmon though. And it turned out it was. And it turned out Sean saw me find out it was, and it turned out as well… that he could sing. And it went:
> *There's nothing I don't believe anymore*
> *Since Sylvia Wist went climbing*
> *Water doesn't run down anymore*
> *My ears are not for sound anymore*
> *My face and my mouth will not frown anymore*
> *Since Sylvia Wist went climbing*
> *Explain away gravity, Sylvia*
> *Make time go backwards, Sylvia*
> *I've forgotten the answers, Sylvia*
> *You've rewritten the answers, Sylvia*
> *Since Sylvia Wist went climbing*
> *I've lost all my faith in timing*

He stood in front of my flat—I was living alone by then—and he played that song through my letter box. And I really liked it. But I didn't come out.

He played it like that for three evenings, after he finished work at Coles, and on the fourth evening, he didn't come. Because he'd gone to the dam, it turned out. Because he thought maybe my impossibilities... were possible.

But of course, it turns out they're not. Not for anyone except me. And Sean Tiernan was found twelve k's away, cold and covered in mud.

So that's why I've got two songs.

SCENE SEVEN

NOAH *sits in a car in silence.*

NOAH: Cars go so quickly now.

And so do words. And so does rain. And so do rivers. Everything goes so fast these days.

Except bridges.

Bridges don't go fast. Bridges are still. They are perfectly still.

I am stepping out of the car and it's dawn and I'm on the bridge. I'm on the bridge and I am standing here and I—

And I am standing here and I am— I am turning in a circle. I am turning in a circle and I'm noticing everything that's around me.

I am noticing a— You notice everything in the mornings—do you think that? I notice everything in the— It's so still.

The marks from my tyres are long and black and they snake along the road. And they finish where the wheels are now.

Of course they do.

Of course they do.

Bristol is so big all below me. But it has no people in it. There are no people here. I'm on the Clifton Bridge and there are—

The car is on the bridge, and the bridge is still.

Ha. And the car is still. And you went through a hole in the windscreen. You went right through a—

I saw you go through and I— But I— I saw you fly right through a hole in the. But I didn't see—

You didn't land. I didn't see you land.

I hear the sirens now, and there are no people here. I sit back in the car. I sit back in your side of the car. I sit in your side. I look through the hole. I saw you fly.

I look through the hole.

Winter

SCENE EIGHT

SYLVIA: In the Winter, when the sun is only a tiny moment of time in Iceland, and the night is long, and the shadows are long, fisherwomen may find themselves sitting by the window, and telling their worries to the tundra.

EMMA: Papa got immensely ill three nights ago. His head was as hot as the stove—honestly, if I put one hand on him and one on the stove, I do not know which would have burnt first. Of course not honestly, but you know.

Ulli and I we call the doctor, but he is far away and without petrol, so we can only do what he says on the telephone. He says to make many flannels wet and to sit these on Papa, on his head and his shoulders and his chest. He says that he will send antibiotics tomorrow, but tomorrow is a thousand years when your one and only papa is as hot as a stove.

Papa is so weak he cannot leave the armchair and his throat is so dry that he coughs over and over and his tongue swells. This makes us double worried and we feed him water through a straw and make turns being there for him, like a good son and a good daughter. We make turns with our sleeping, Ulli and me.

And you think maybe: 'Are you scared to sleep, because another time when you did, Paddy Blue Skin went to death'. But this is nonsense. I have slept a thousand times since then, and sometimes I wake up to sunshine and sometimes to rain. But never again to death. Sleep does not equal death and if you think this, you would grow big bags under your eyes pretty quickly and all you would have is nightmares.

I wake up in the morning and Ulli is doing an unusual thing. He has Mama's old scissors and he is cutting off Papa's big beard. Papa lies back in the armchair watching Ulli's face and Ulli looks immensely focused. And I can see how great an idea this is, because Papa he is so hot and a beard it makes you hotter and now it is going, falling onto his bare chest in great, grey curls. And I have only ever known Papa as a bearded man. But today, right now… he is someone else. He has a chin that I have never met and his cheeks are round—I always thought his head was large because of the hair.

But his head is large.

'You have no beard', I tell my Papa. And he and Ulli stop and look at me, my brother and a new man looking at me. And Papa coughs, and gasps for some breath, and wipes his hand through the dirty mat of chopped-off hair stuck to his sweaty, large cheeks. And he says:

PAPA: You and Ulli are taking the boat out today.

SCENE NINE

A rooftop garden.

SYLVIA: In Bristol the heartbroken man will walk up and down the rows that separate the beds of the rooftop garden. He walks—

NOAH: Slowly and without purpose. But when there's a weed growing, I pick the weed. And if the twine round the strawberries has frayed or broken, I'll pull some more from my pocket and fix that.

In the Winter, I think of Sophia flying through the air, and in the Winter I think of me and my sadness without her. But that's okay—'cause if you love someone and they make you feel happy, you love that feeling, 'cause it's from them. And same with sad—if it's a person you love who gives you that, then… it can be a good thing. It's all just a way of remembering.

SYLVIA: Sometimes in the Winter, the whole garden is just Noah's, because people go straight home from work to avoid the cold, and they ask if they can do less volunteering. And he always says yes. And quietly, he's happy with that.

NOAH: But this Winter, the big Australian man is there all the time too. Luckily, he's not much of a talker though.

CALEB: Hello.

Beat.

NOAH: And he smiles at me, like he's a bit chuffed, because he knows lots of the volunteers aren't coming, 'cause of the cold, but he still is. And of course I can't tell him there's something wrong with that—because it is a community garden, and because he is trying to help.

Hello.

CALEB: Noah looks relieved to see me.

NOAH: But secretly I wish he'd go away.

Beat.

You not getting cold?

CALEB: The gloves are good in a few ways—with the thorns, and the chill too. You're not wearing any.

NOAH: Tough hands.

CALEB: You've been doing this a long time.

NOAH: Mm.

CALEB: Hope I get good like you soon. I'm not much good at gardening am I?

NOAH: You're alright—only good gardener's nature. Rest of us just get in the way.

Silence. They stand together in the cold.

You living here now?

CALEB: Ha—not sure. My aunty lives here—lived here—in the building, Number Eight, so I came to visit her. And then she died pretty soon after that.

NOAH: Oh.

CALEB: But she left me her flat.

NOAH: Oh.

CALEB: Which is really lovely. But, you know, lovelier with her in it.

NOAH: Course. [*Pause.*] How did she—

CALEB: Die. Old. Being old.

Beat.

I was talking to her at the time. Because she sat with her eyes closed a lot. And she'd just go... *hmmm* sometimes. But this time she didn't. For about twenty minutes. And I was talking about a dream, this lift dream I had, and it was quite an interesting dream. I thought. So I just kept on talking about it. And yeah, after about twenty minutes her cat jumped on her lap. And that was when her head, dropped... sideways. That's how I knew. That she was dead.

NOAH: Right. [*Pause.*] I'm sorry.

CALEB: What do you do?

What *do* you do, Noah—in general?

NOAH: I garden.
CALEB: Yeah. And… you got a girlfriend?
NOAH: Wife.
CALEB: But she doesn't garden?

Pause.

NOAH: Not anymore.

SCENE TEN

A car. ELISE *drives as a baby cries.*

ELISE: You are the loudest baby I think I have ever met, Jacob. You have so strong lungs, don't you? You are so annoying aren't you?

You are not annoying. But you are odd… my odd baby. You are odd not liking the lovely bed your papa and I buy for you. Is something wrong with your bed? Or with your brain? Can you not know a bed is for sleeping? A bed is for sleeping, *mein Liebling*— can your brain not know this?

Oh no—did your brain break when you were born, Jacob? Oh no, how awful. Don't tell your father. It will make him so sad.

Silence.

While we are on the subject of secrets, Jacob, while we are driving to Braunschweig, and it is the middle of the night, do you mind if I… You must keep this so quiet please. Please—I trust you. Please, *ja*?

Pause.

His name is Georg. Yes, that Georg! I know, that is the thing. With the hair, yes—I always say to your papa: 'Please my lover, don't grow your hair too long. That is for young men, and you are old now, and you have a beautiful fat belly that means you are old now. *Kurz bitte—kurz*'.

But Georg, his hair is everything I say no about. It is so funny. And of course he has a belly too, I know. Everything is upside-down now. *Ja*, everything…

Beat.

And... I am feeling the dragons again, Jacob. I am feeling this...
this passion inside of me. And it is warm. And real. I am feeling
real again, Jacob, you know—solid, like here— [*She taps the
dashboard.*] this is a real thing and it... it makes a sound, it... it
leaves an imprint in the leaves, you know...
And maybe for a time I've been feeling... not so real. A ghost. A
ghost driving with a half-ghost baby (because your father is human,
I'm sure of this). But me... always tired, always disappearing. A
little more every day.

Beat.

And now Georg! And now... [*She taps the dash again.*] This, you
know! Now this is again! Now your Mutti is filling up again, Jacob. Is...
There are no words for it. I've found my love.

Silence.

And now you pretend to sleep. How funny. How funny your timing
is, *Liebling*. Okay then, you pretend to sleep and I keep driving. I
will turn round in Braunschweig. I will turn round outside the first
house your papa and me bought for each other. I will look at the
house and then I will turn round.

Sleep tight, *mein Liebling*. Sleep tight, my poor broken-brained
child.

SCENE ELEVEN

EMMA: We stand in the boat together, Ulli and me, Emma the Greek.
And I say: 'Your knots in the net are the shittest knots I have seen
in a million years. I think all the fish are swimming right through
the big stupid holes you have left and telling their friends that you
are a retard, Ulli'.
And Ulli says... nothing. Which is the great pleasure of ridiculing
my brother. He will say not one word back at you. He throws a
mackerel at my head though and it gives me a black eye. And if I
was a proper girl, like who wore make-up and had boyfriends and
did not leave school at fourteen to fish with her papa, I would have
cried. But instead I just spit over the side and say: 'Fuck you'. Then
we fish together all afternoon and until it is dark.

In the nighttime, we play cards and drink whisky and talk about Papa. And the way we talk (seeing Ulli has a black hole and saves his voice for very very little) is I say things and Ulli nods or shakes or flicks me with a card or pours more whisky. Or he writes on paper sometimes.

We neither of us can believe that Papa is not sitting in this boat. He is his boat and he is captain and hard worker and a taskmaster. And in my years, which is nineteen, he has never missed a work day. He always was home for four days and away for four days. And home for four days. And away. And when each of us was becoming fourteen, we do this with him—four days, and four days, and four days, for always. Paddy Blue Skin only got to do one four days, because the cold it killed him and he sleeps with Mama now… for all the days.

I pick my nose for a bit while Ulli writes. And then he shows me the paper and it says: 'This morning, when he was in the doorway, with no beard and the blanket around him like the old woman, I felt like he was younger than us and we are the parents and he is the kid'. And I say maybe he is like Samson, from the Bible, and Ulli has made him weak by taking his hair. And Ulli hits me with an ashtray and I spit whisky in his eyes so he screams (he can still scream). And then we go to bed.

In the night I dream about the thing my mama told me once, that there is a house in the woods where every man of one family for fourteen generations has gone to die.

A MAN *smokes, readying for death.*

I imagine them all there, over hundreds of years, arriving at the house, one at a time, alone, and knowing this is the end. And knowing they will see the end alone. And smoking cigarettes.

SYLVIA *appears and she and the* MAN *watch each other in silence. He offers her a cigarette. She declines. A moment. She is gone.*

I wake up and it is four in the morning and the waves are rough and Ulli's bed is empty. I walk onto the deck and here he is. He has been going for a piss off the boat and a large wave has arrived from out of the darkness and my brother has tripped over backwards and fallen onto the jag. He is lying on the deck and even though he is on top of it, I can see the jag hook because it is coming out through this chest hole that is new. Blood is coming out of his mouth and, just as rare, words are coming out of his mouth too.

ULLI: I fell onto the jag. It is inside me, Emma the Greek. It is going through me. I can feel when my heart pumps, it pushes against the metal—boom, boom, like this, just here. You are the last thing I will see, little sister. And you were also the last thing Paddy Blue Skin saw before he went to Mama. And that Mama saw before she went to the sea.

AND maybe Papa too, when you see him, it will be the last thing. Because you are a terrible magic, Emma the Greek. You carry death with you. You carry it and... [*Gasping suddenly*] I literally just felt... my heart explode against... the metal... it is...

Silence. EMMA *stares at her brother's still form.*

SCENE TWELVE

SYLVIA *stands somewhere.*

SYLVIA: Ah! Okay... The first thing you do is check for danger. I'm not in the middle of a road. I'm not on the edge of something. There's not... fire nearby—or a person nearby.

You get your bearings. You look at the clues of a space. So: this is a... small room, that's an old chair, that's a kite. Those are newspapers. It's *night*—it's dark outside the window. So okay, you work out... I'm in the northern hemisphere. Okay.

CALEB *shifts in his sleep.* SYLVIA *is startled, but goes over. She recognises him from the lift, watches him, then leans in and kisses him. He is startled awake. Pause.*

CALEB: Lift girl. [*Beat.*] You didn't disappear.
SYLVIA: No.
CALEB: We were kissing.
SYLVIA: Yes.
CALEB: Are you my auntie?
SYLVIA: What!?

CALEB: I don't know. We... she just died. I thought you were her... when she was younger—a young ghost.

SYLVIA: We were kissing.

CALEB: Yeah, that seemed strange.

SYLVIA: That is strange.

CALEB: You were in my lift too. At work, at my old work in Australia. That was you.

SYLVIA: It felt closer.

CALEB: I moved. I'm in Bristol now—at my auntie's.

SYLVIA: The one that died.

CALEB: That's why I thought—

SYLVIA: I'm not your auntie—

CALEB: Yeah. That's good. [*Beat.*] How are you... doing this—being here?

SYLVIA: [*distracted*] I've never visited the same person twice.

CALEB: I rarely get visited at all! By anyone. Once or twice. Hardly ever twice.
  I can't believe... Lift Girl.

SYLVIA: Sylvia.

CALEB: Caleb.
  So... am I not asleep? I feel awake. My water bottle's gone cold. You must be cold. Do you want to—

SYLVIA: Is that alright?

CALEB: Yeah!

She climbs into bed beside him. They sit there. Silence.

  Is it okay if... if I'm not sure whether you're real or not?

SYLVIA: Fine.

CALEB: And I don't even... ask? Or try to find out? 'Cause, like... I could feel amazed about, you know, a dream woman *materialising* in my bedroom. Or I could just feel amazed about... there being a woman in my bedroom. They're both a bit unbelievable.

SYLVIA: Well go with the second one then.

CALEB: Yeah. [*Pause.*] I'm awake now—do you want a cup of tea?

SYLVIA: Sure.

He hops out of bed, revealing childish pyjamas.

CALEB: How'd you have it?

SYLVIA: White with one.

CALEB: Ha. We're the same.

He exits. SYLVIA *sits in bed. Silence.*

SCENE THIRTEEN

EMMA: I roll up my brother in some bedsheets. But before I cover his face, I give him a chance, to say anything else to me, any last thing that is not about me carrying death. But Ulli is silent. Ulli is nearly always silent. I lift him up with my strength and give him to the ocean.

And then I drink all the whisky, and think about Papa. And think about what I carry with me. And think about how to keep him alive.

Spring

SCENE FOURTEEN

SYLVIA: In Spring late at night, the German countryside is a web of roads that weave and dip, beside slow-flowing rivers, and heavy trees. In the daytime, it's all these things too. But at night the river flows slower, the trees seem heavier.

It's all just a trick of the eyes.

ELISE *drives.*

ELISE: I wish so much I did not love you, Jacob. I wish I was a horror mother and I could place you in a bin. Or I wish I could wrap you in a blanket and leave you on a step for the nuns to find. But I don't think they do that anymore, I'm not sure.

And I think, sadly, I love you too much to share you with anyone.

I think also—no, I know—I love your father too. So much as I love you, I love him. I love you because… you were inside me. And so now we are connected forever—your blood and my blood flowed together once, and now always more we are tied, you and me.

But your father I love because we share no blood, but instead time. So much time, Jacob. We know when to wake, and when to sleep. We know this together.

Some people say— my friend Connie says (you know Connie— *ja,* with the glasses) Connie says time is the worst thing to share with a man and this is why Werner and her live apart. But this is bullshit—Connie just doesn't love Werner. She loves his money and she loves antiques and she loves cigarettes and she loves galleries. But she doesn't know about loving a man.

I do, Jacob. I know about loving a man so much. Once, is ten years ago now, I danced with your father, with Matthias, in the square. I wear the most beautiful green dress that my Oma won in a game of cards. And I twirl Matthias like he is the woman. And we put our heads back and we close our eyes and we spin. And we did not care if people saw. This is love.

Silence.

And now here is a new kind of love happening. It is called loving my husband so much that even if I start to love another man—a man with long hair called Georg… I cannot stop loving the first one.

This means it is very true love, Jacob, very real love. But it does not mean it is easy love.

If I could walk away from you, and from your father, and walk across to Georg and sleep with him, then love is easy. But I cannot.

Because love is not an exchange, one for the other, *ja*? Love is an… accumulation. Loves can pile up until our arms are full, Jacob. But loves cannot be switched off.

Or at least mine cannot.

Pause.

Can you please now learn to speak, *mein Liebling*, so you can tell me the answer? I am waiting.

Silence.

SCENE FIFTEEN

CALEB *and* NOAH *work in the garden.*

CALEB: I want to get a tattoo.

NOAH: Why—what of?

CALEB: A dragon. A dragon… going across my back, up my neck.

NOAH: Why a dragon?

CALEB: People are scared of dragons. Used to make sacrifices to them—give cows to them. Asian warriors used to have heaps of dragon tattoos.

NOAH: Yeah, but… you're not Asian. Or scary—are you Caleb? You collect teapots. You wear ankle socks.

CALEB: 'Cause my feet sweat—

NOAH: I know why you do it. I'm just saying… you're not scary.

CALEB: No. [*Beat.*] I was thinking a dragon or a skull.

NOAH: Oh god. Go a dragon then.

CALEB: So you like dragon?

NOAH: Only more than a skull. If you said… dragon or swastika, I'd go for dragon as well. Dragon or… shotgun. Dragon or penis. Don't get a penis tattoo.

CALEB: I wasn't going to.

NOAH: That's good.

Although the dragon might have a penis. You might see the dragon's penis in the larger dragon tattoo.

CALEB: But that's okay—incidental penis is okay.

NOAH: Oh for sure. Penis in context is fine. Just… not solo penis.

CALEB: No.

NOAH: No.

Beat.

CALEB: Are dragons male then—

NOAH: Dragons… don't exist, Caleb. They're genderless. Or they're whatever gender you fancy.

CALEB: Mm. [*Beat.*] Male. I reckon a male one.

NOAH: Sure. Or of course you could avoid the genitals altogether. Leave that to the imagination.

CALEB: Oh, I will, yeah—but male if people ask.

NOAH: You think… people will ask, then?

CALEB: Probably not. But you can't be too careful hey.

NOAH: Oh with dragon genders, absolutely not. [*Beat.*] You're hilarious.

CALEB: What?

NOAH: Nothing, Caleb. Nothing at all.

SCENE SIXTEEN

EMMA: My four days has become four weeks. I have made my decision and it is to stay on the water forever. Ulli, as well as being an annoying brother and a poor net fixer and now a dead man, was also correct. I have been the last to see three of my family already and Papa, I can kill him too. He is sick already, he has no beard anymore, he cannot fish. And if I set my foot on land, I think yes, he will die.

And so I will sail, for the rest of my days. I will not touch a port, in case my Papa dies then. I will flow everywhere but never stop. I will get my water… by collecting the rain. I will eat fish— so many fish that I will become a fish. This is a bad joke. I will eat other things. I will trade with others for things. But land—no. Land is something I will say goodbye to, forever. Because land is the death of my Papa now—if I meet land, I meet my Papa's death.

And so this journey at sea, it must be my Papa's life. And I will sail for a long time. I will give my Papa a long life.

SCENE SEVENTEEN

SYLVIA *and* CALEB *lie in bed. They smile at each other. Silence.*

CALEB: Was that good?

SYLVIA: You can't ask that!

CALEB: Why not?

SYLVIA: You can *say* that was good. You can say *I* was good. But you can't ask.

CALEB: Okay. [*Beat.*] That was good—

SYLVIA: Well you can't say it now. I just heard you ask—you're not really sure.

CALEB: I am! I thought it was very good, great in fact—I thought it was great. I just... Sex isn't a... daily event for me—

SYLVIA: And don't say event. It's like a, a school fair, or a... swimming carnival.

CALEB: Don't say *event*. Don't ask if it was good—

SYLVIA: Don't take notes!

CALEB: No—I won't. Sorry. I'm nervous.

SYLVIA: It was good.

CALEB: Yeah—yeah it was. I was... in control.

SYLVIA: ...

CALEB: I'm usually... With my hobbies, it's usually people instructing me, you know—the firearms officer, the Afghan kite guy. But that— that was *me*, you know. That was me leading it—

SYLVIA: Can we please not talk about it anymore?

CALEB: Yeah, sure. [*Beat.*] What I'm saying is—

SYLVIA: You're still talking about it—

CALEB: Last bit. What I'm saying is... I usually feel... *in need of* instruction. It's not just coming from them. It's me—

'Cept for my piano teacher. That was *really* about her. Like, she had huge dominance issues. She *shouted* at me—she used to shout. I'm a grown man. She's shouting at me. I had to leave. [*Beat.*] Where was—

SYLVIA: It's you—

CALEB: It's me... Not knowing what, what I should be doing. Or how I should be doing what I'm doing.

But with you it's not like that, Sylvia. I don't feel that I need instruction. I don't feel like I don't know what I'm doing. I know what I'm doing.

SYLVIA: Me.

CALEB: Yeah.

SYLVIA: You're doing me.

CALEB: I was just before.

SYLVIA: But now you're talking.

CALEB: Less than usual. Usually I babble.

SYLVIA: You sound babbly. But... I don't mind. 'Cause you're nice. And you make me feel like I know what I'm doing too.

Beat.

CALEB: Which is?

SYLVIA: You.

CALEB: Now? Again?

SYLVIA: If you wouldn't mind.

She climbs on top of him.

CALEB: Have you ever disappeared during—

SYLVIA: No. Stop talking now.

CALEB: Okay.

> NOAH *lies in bed, alone, and listens to* CALEB *and* SYLVIA's *loud and enthusiastic sex. He stares at the ceiling and becomes increasingly frustrated. Eventually, he turns to a photo of Sophia on his left and can only laugh, exasperated. He stares at her a long time, then returns his gaze to the ceiling.*

SCENE EIGHTEEN

ELISE *is driving, a phone pressed to her ear.*

ELISE: He has just gone quiet, two minutes ago. It's the river—he likes the sound of it, of the water. Now he is snoring.

Because I don't mind the driving.

Because I sleep enough. In the mornings Matthias gets up too early, but not me. He leaves me—he lets me sleep, every day. He is a good man.

Ja you are too but... I think he is better.

Lots of reasons... If Matthias cuts two pieces of bread, and one is a funny cut (like too thin, the knife went sideways) and the other is even, he will give me that one. And with wine, he always fills my glass first and then himself. If—

No there is more, I am telling you more. If we are in a, a shop and the shopkeeper is rude to us or to me or to him, Matthias later on says: 'I bet she had a bad day. I wonder what happened to her'. And if it was me saying it or you saying it, we would say: 'What a fucking bitch. I only want cigarettes, and she looks at me like a leper. Fuck her'.

Ja, you would. And that is okay—that makes us human. But it does not make us good. It does not make us as good as Matthias.

Beat.

No.

No—I am driving tonight, to make my son fall asleep, and now he is asleep, and so now we go home. Home to his father. Home to my Matthias.

No.

Because—god, you shit me Georg—because if I am driving to you, then I am not driving for my son, for getting my son to sleep. Then I am only driving to be with you. And for this I do not need Jacob. For this I just need to pack a bag, and tell Matthias, and tell Jacob, and go. If I was driving to you, then I would drive to you.

No. That is not the reason I drive.

Ja, I love you.

Ja, we love each other! Okay good, so what? Love is not a... a solution word—is not a magic answer. Not *Abracadabra*. It does not... Nothing disappears when you say it. I don't say: 'I love you', and poof—there is my son gone. There is my good husband gone. I am a single woman suddenly and here is Georg and... we kiss and... Take a bow—the magic show is over. Great.

Well if you do I feel sorry for you.

Beat.

No. I have not lost hope.

Because.

Because I remember how it feels to lie with you on the leaves. Because I remember a lot of things. But I do not do magic tricks, Georg. And I do not make good men disappear.

Beat.

And we have been at dinner parties together, you and me and Matthias, for eight years, so many dinner parties. And you have *never* poured my wine first. Not before you loved me—and not since.

A pause. ELISE *hangs up the phone. She winds down the window and is lulled by the sound of the water.*

The sound pervades all spaces, as the stars come out and all stare up, distracted. ELISE *stares up through the windscreen, and steers.* EMMA *stares from atop the swaying deck and releases the net.* NOAH *rises and takes to the roof garden. He stares up, while winding twine.* SYLVIA *finds herself somewhere and is initially shocked, but then stares, at peace.* CALEB *wakes and finds Sylvia gone. He is saddened, then reconciles himself to rising and ascending the stairs. In the garden he finds* NOAH.

NOAH: Can't sleep either?

CALEB: [*shaking his head*] Want a hand?

NOAH: Thanks.

The two begin spooling the twine together then stop, distracted, and stare up.

INTERVAL

Summer

SCENE NINETEEN

The rooftop garden—a hot day. CALEB *and* NOAH *work.*

SYLVIA: In the Summer, Caleb will dig at the beds of the community garden and break up the soil with a small hoe. He whistles while he does this and, for the first time in a long time, feels content. He's found he's *good* at something—not a lot, not much, just one thing.

And he's found as well that someone who's good *at* something…

CALEB: Can then help others—can then be good *for* something.

And so I help. I help the children plant, and I help the old people carry. And on Thursdays I help chop carrots for the large community lunch. And once a month I help takes notes at the rooftop garden meeting. When it rains, I bound up the stairs and help bring washing in. And when the fireworks perform their dance across the sky—like flames pouring from the mouths of dragons—I help to add to the collective cheer… by being just one more smiling, shiny-eyed face—nothing special—just one more person, staring up, shoulder-to-shoulder with my neighbours.

[*To* NOAH] I'm gonna have lunch. You want something?

NOAH: Nah, all good. See you later.

CALEB: Mm.

He rises, pats NOAH's *back and exits.* NOAH *continues to work.* SYLVIA *enters, unheard, wearing Caleb's pyjamas. She watches him.*

SYLVIA: You're Noah—Noah who works in the garden.

NOAH: You're… a girl in Caleb's pyjamas. He just went for lunch.

SYLVIA: Oh.

NOAH: You his girlfriend then?

SYLVIA: Friend. The garden looks amazing.

NOAH: Summertime. Makes everything look nice. You know about plants?

SYLVIA: Not these ones. I live in Australia—up north. It's hot. Different.

NOAH: You travelling then?

SYLVIA: Yeah.

NOAH: How long for?

SYLVIA: Not sure. Not long.

NOAH: Caleb's a nice guy, isn't he?

SYLVIA: He's lovely.

Beat.

NOAH: You heard about his dragon tattoo—

SYLVIA: Oh my god! And he said you got him all worried about the dick.

NOAH: I was just winding him up.

SYLVIA: He's stressed about it now. He printed out these pictures from the Net and—

NOAH: He's really getting it?

SYLVIA: Mm.

NOAH: Wow.

Beat.

SYLVIA: He told me about your wife.

NOAH: Oh yeah?

SYLVIA: I'm really sorry.

NOAH: Thanks.

Beat.

SYLVIA: I'm an orphan.

NOAH: Oh right. [*Pause.*] Is that the ratio then?

SYLVIA: What?

NOAH: Two parents—does that equal one wife? Like, are we swapping death statistics? Are we friends now?

SYLVIA: Okay. Forget it then.

NOAH: Or are you in the lead? Yeah of course, you had two die—my mistake, sorry.

SYLVIA: Caleb said you were nice.

NOAH: Caleb's a good man—he thinks everyone's nice. You want to leave me to my weeding now?

Beat.

SYLVIA: You should sort your shit out—

NOAH: Excellent! I'll do that now, yeah. Got widowed at twenty-two. Went quietly about my business for a while, gardening, you know.

And then one magical day, some random Australian chick pries into my stuff and... she works me out! And then suddenly I can let my grief go. Oh wow, I can feel it already. That is a massive fucking relief—

SYLVIA: Fuck you.

NOAH: Fuck you. Get out of my garden.

SYLVIA: It's a communal garden.

NOAH: Yeah and you're not part of the community. Sleeping with a simpleton doesn't get you in—

She knocks the plant out of his hand.

Hey!—

SYLVIA: Cunt.

She storms off. NOAH *is left with a pile of dirt.*

SCENE TWENTY

EMMA: It is March fourteenth. I have been sailing for three years now. In that time I have met no other boats. A few times I have seen them, but always I sail away quickly so nobody dies. It is no bother—I catch the rainwater and I eat the fish. I watch the horizon and I write songs. Ulli left a guitar on the boat and I have learnt this instrument. I am a wonderful guitar woman now, truly amazing. Papa lives on in his house, I hope, and is not feeling sick anymore, I hope. The land calls me sometimes, but I ignore it.

Today it is March fourteenth and I am at latitude fourteen, longitude twenty-two, and the sun has come up. The sun has come up on hundreds of dead men, all lying in the sea. Some are on their back and some are on their front. Some are close and some lie very alone, like they did not wish to share their dying with anyone else. One holds a ring and the ring says *The Orkney*: this was the name of their ship. The ring did this man no good though—he is dead also. It is the cold that killed them, I could have told them that. But now I do not have to. They know.

For two days, I sail amongst them with a long rope, making loops and tying each at the hand. I do this altogether 235 times until there is the longest line of bodies floating behind my Papa's fishing boat. I do not know so much why I have done this. But I do know it feels better than having each man float in his own direction. And the sharks come around and nibble at one, and then the other, a little bit at one man, a whole body of his friend.

Then I realise the answer and I take the anchor from my papa's boat and tie it to the end of the long line of dead men who were once the crew of *The Orkney*. I have no need anymore for this anchor, as it is for stopping and I cannot stop. So I give it to the men and they disappear one at a time in a long line, with their one hand out in front of them—*goodbye, goodbye, goodbye*. And then they are all floating down, down to the sea where my Mama and Paddy Blue Skin and Ulli wait to greet them. And I write a message for her and tie it to the rope, for them to deliver. But I will not tell you what it says—it is words between a daughter and a Mama, and you do not need to hear.

Then I sail away and return to the things I am good at.

Maybe a problem is people try to be good at too much. They maybe do not achieve this and they get sad. But me, I am good at only three things—catching fish, playing guitar and killing every one I meet. And two of these I could do forever with a smile on my face—honestly, you would not believe my pleasure. But the other one… this is no joy. I wish very much that I did not possess this talent. And then maybe I could go home.

SCENE TWENTY-ONE

ELISE *and* SYLVIA *sit together in the car, roaring, crying with laughter.*

ELISE: Hang on—one second. Sorry.

She pulls over the car and catches her breath.

Did he get his job back?

SYLVIA: No. How could he? What do you say? 'Sorry I came in your lift.'

ELISE: *Ja*! Ha! [*She calms down.*] This was… this is a really funny thing. A funny man.

SYLVIA: I think we woke your kid up.

ELISE: Ah, always. He wakes up, and then asleep again. Sometime later awake. After, sleeping. On and on, you know.

SYLVIA: And… nice to wake up to laughter.

ELISE: *Stimmt.* I keep driving?

SYLVIA: Sure.

> *She does.*

ELISE: You have no interest in where we go?

SYLVIA: It *is* interesting. I just… don't mind. Wherever you need to go and… I'll just head on from there.

ELISE: Because… you are hitchhiking?

SYLVIA: Yes.

ELISE: Hitchhiking, but… with no luggage.

SYLVIA: Mm.

> *Beat.*

ELISE: Sylvia… You did not, did not now really just … appear from nowhere in my car, did you?

SYLVIA: No—

ELISE: I am tired, driving like this at night—I do it lots of nights, and I am tired and… I am sure I forget bits, forget things. So… I *forgot* picking you up, *ja?*

SYLVIA: I guess so.

ELISE: Because… people do not, just appear in cars do they?

SYLVIA: It'd be a good trick.

ELISE: It would. It would be an amazing trick.

> *Beat.*

ELISE: Okay! Tell me more—what else does the tall man do?

SYLVIA: Um… Alright…

He told me he wanted to join the army (ha—this is great actually). And when you go to sign up, in Australia, they do, you know, an interview. And one question was why he wanted to join. And he said he was inspired by selfless people—he said he'd like to win a medal one day for being selfless.

ELISE: Ha. A medal for selfless—this is funny already.

SYLVIA: Yeah I know. And the interviewer asked him which one, which medal he wanted. And the only one he could think of, was the

Dickin Medal.

ELISE: Dickin Medal?

SYLVIA: Mm—one he read about. So he said that. And…

She starts laughing.

ELISE: *Ja?*

SYLVIA: The Dickin Medal—it's the medal for animals. For really brave animals in war. Like… like dolphins, you know with the bombs—

ELISE: *Ja*, they carry the bombs to the submarine.

SYLVIA: Yeah. And… [*Laughing*] And pigeons—the first ever Dickin Medal went to a pigeon, he said. And he'd just… *forgotten* that bit when he said it.

The laughter builds between them.

ELISE: He is an idiot!

SYLVIA: Mm. And then… everyone found out. And through all his training (he never passed but he did the training) that was his nickname: Pigeon. And (ha!) They used to tape messages to his leg when he was asleep!

ELISE: Is so stupid.

SYLVIA: Yeah—like a courier pigeon. They actually made him carry them to people. It was awful—I'm not laughing. [*She is.*] And… ha! There was—

CALEB: There was this big statue, in the parade ground, of a colonel. And they put this sign on it that said: 'Fuck off Pigeon—stop shitting on my head'—

Both women explode in laugh. CALEB *is oblivious.*

'Cause they swear a lot in the army. And… Oh, heaps of stuff—they used to give me birdseed, in the canteen—bits of apple, stuff like that. And the drill-sergeant made me do my own march—you know, with the head [*He demonstrates.*] Yeah, like a pigeon. Stop laughing.

SYLVIA: I'm not.

CALEB: And when I got discharged, they gave me it.

SYLVIA: Gave you what?

CALEB: The Dickin Medal—

Both women burst out laughing.

They said I earned it.

SYLVIA: They said he earned it! He is... (Ow, I'm hurting.) He still is the only human being, in the world, to officially receive the Dickin Medal!

ELISE: Ha! So good! This man is... like a child in his brain.

SYLVIA: Ha... [*Beat.*] But nah—he's not. He's just... unlucky. And sweet.

Some people they... they kind of *collect up* the unluckiness for the rest of us, you know. And the really good ones... They don't even complain about it. They just take it. And they carry on.

You reckon?

ELISE: I... I am only just learning about good men now. About how to recognise them. But *ja*—you are right with how you say it. [*Beat.*] You really do not mind where we go?

SYLVIA: No, Elise. I'll be gone soon anyway.

Pause.

ELISE: Gone—what does this mean?

SYLVIA: Just... Don't be scared when it happens, okay. Just... keep watching the road, okay. Don't... Just watch the road.

Beat.

ELISE: Okay.

SYLVIA: And thank you. Thanks for the laugh. It felt good.

ELISE: Is... okay. [*Pause.*] Are you really going t—

SYLVIA: Just watch the road Elise... Just keep watching it.

Both stare ahead as they drive on in silence.

SCENE TWENTY-TWO

CALEB *and* NOAH *are leaning on rakes, in the sun.*

NOAH: I don't really understand any part of what you just said.

CALEB: Look, it's simple. I am alive. And you are alive. And our *lives*... are nothing special.

NOAH: Thanks.

CALEB: In a good way.

NOAH: Oh.

CALEB: 'Cause *nothing special* means we're real, yeah. That's what real, alive people are: nothing special. But *special people*: they're kind of... not alive, not like you and me. They're something else. They... transcend things.

NOAH: But... Sophia, she was... *really* special. And she was alive.

CALEB: Yeah—she *was*. But now she's not anymore. Special people like that, like her, see, they can't just... carry on. They can't just waste their time walking among the *nothing special* people... Like us, like all of us—getting old, getting boring.

NOAH: So what are you saying? What's that mean about the accident?

CALEB: I'm saying... *Accident* might not be the right word for it.

NOAH: Don't do that. She's... Don't talk about the dead like that—

CALEB: But, hear me out. I'm saying... *Dead* might not be the right word either.

NOAH: ...

CALEB: 'Cause look...

You didn't see her land. Did you? You didn't bury her. You didn't... identify her body... scatter her ashes. You never saw her again.

And dead—*being dead*—it has rules. All those things are rules—you see them, you bury them, you say goodbye: rules. All I'm saying is... she doesn't fit any of the rules.

Beat.

NOAH: So what *are* you saying, you twat?

CALEB: I'm saying... Maybe there's another thing. Maybe there's not just *alive* and *dead*. Like how we decide everyone's one of those, or the other one.

But maybe there's a third place.

SYLVIA *wakes, standing in a castle's ruins. Horses surround her. None are afraid. Silence.*

NOAH: A third place?

CALEB: Yeah. Like, she went from here, from *Alive*. And she went *there*. Not to death—to the third place. 'Cause you saw her fly, yeah. But you didn't see her land. And landing: that means alive or dead.

You land, and you're one or you're the other. But *not landing*… That's something else.

Silence.

NOAH: You're the worst thing that's ever happened to me, Caleb.

Beat.

CALEB: Yeah. Yeah, I get that sometimes.

Autumn

SCENE TWENTY-THREE

SYLVIA: Autumn is a time for travelling, where other seasons are not. In Autumn, things fly off trees, and float down streams, and waft, and roam.
In Winter all is frozen still. In Summer it's too hot to move. Spring's for new beginnings, and discovering where you've arrived, not where you'll go. That's for Autumn. In Autumn, the clever ones travel.

Each is seen in a state of motion: NOAH *stands with thumb outstretched;* CALEB *does up a ludicrous, tight wetsuit;* ELISE *angrily packs a bag;* SYLVIA *wakes somewhere;* EMMA *steers her trawler and sings to herself.*

EMMA: *There's nothing I don't believe anymore*
Since Sylvia Wist went climbing
Water doesn't run down anymore
My ears are not for sound anymore
My face and my mouth will not frown anymore
Since Sylvia Wist went climbing
Explain away gravity, Sylvia
Make time go backwards, Sylvia
I've forgotten the answers, Sylvia
You've rewritten the answers, Sylvia
Since Sylvia Wist went climbing
I've lost all my faith in timing
Silence.

Sometimes we do not understand the songs we invent.

SCENE TWENTY-FOUR

ELISE *angrily straps* JACOB *into his baby seat. A man is seen/ heard/ alluded to.*

MATTHIAS: *Also jetzt gehst du—* [English: So now you're going—]
ELISE: *Ja*, fuck you! Fuck you Matthias! I have never! I have never done a thing with him! I could have—a hundred times I could have! But fuck you Matthias, I didn't.

MATTHIAS: *Wo gehst du dann!?* [English: So where are you going?]

ELISE: Is none of your business! I am driving! I am forever going driving—you have given me a son that never sleeps, and so together we are driving, always!

MATTHIAS: *Lass ihm hier bleiben!* [English: Leave him here!]

ELISE: No fuck you. You go back to your bed, to your sleep—Jacob comes with me.

She is in the car. Knocking at the window is heard.

Lass Mich in ruhe! [English: Leave me alone/in silence!]

She drives off.

SCENE TWENTY-FIVE

CALEB, *dressed in the wetsuit, packs feverishly.*

CALEB: I used to do so much, in my old life, my full life. 'Cause that's what I thought happy lives had to be—*full*. Except I wasn't—*happy*. And then suddenly… the fullness left. And it turns out happy lives are actually really simple.

   Like, I went from forty-five associations: from tango, and lacrosse… outback survival, introduction to ice sculpture, guitar, piano, air cadets, blind cricket (that was bad). All this stuff. And then all simplified, to just a few things: to Gardening. And The Community. And Noah.

   And Sylvia Wist. I'd just be lying in bed and there she was. This *perfect* woman who always turns up at the *perfect* time and just… is *perfect*. A perfect life where the simpler it got, the better it got.

   And then Noah goes travelling!

   NOAH *is given a lift by* ELISE. *He sits and talks to her, inaudible.*

He gets the idea he's got to hitch across Europe and track down a disappeared dead woman, which is beautiful. But then here's me—with a disappeared alive one! And I realise I should probably do the same.

   Oh yes, my dear Sylvia—no more you visiting me, no more waiting! Now Caleb Prosser… is coming to you! Yes he is! And he's not doing it in a normal way—oh no, he's not! 'Cause Caleb Prosser does not. Do. Normal!

He is *swimming* to you!

Impossible, you say. [*Beat.*] And yes, that is true—England to Australia is truly impossible. But! What about: Fly to Cairns and then swim *the last bit*, to Innisfail? Slightly more possible. Very possible in fact! Seventy-five ks and what's that? I've taken diving lessons before. I'm always at the pool. I did a charity swim when I was at Uni, to raise money for asthma stuff. [*Beat.*] It was a relay, but I did my bit. [*Beat.*] I did most of my bit and... Don't even have asthma! Nothing in it for me, so... pure charity.

But now the tables turn. Now Sylvia will be sitting in *her* flat, in *her* town, looking out over *her* beach and what's this? Maybe her dream guy's gonna appear out of nowhere... for *her*. Come climbing out of the surf—maybe in a bit of a Daniel Craig, Bondy way...

And that's it. That's love. [*Beat.*] And suddenly everything, absolutely everything, feels okay... Because of her.

He dives.

SCENE TWENTY-SIX

EMMA *steers the boat and hears a noise. She turns and sees* SYLVIA *standing on the boat. They watch each other.*

EMMA: There is this... lady on my boat. I am alone, far at sea, and now here is a lady.

SYLVIA: Hello.

EMMA: You did not do this normally. I would have heard you climb on. And you are not wet so... you did not come from the ocean. And I have entered no port, so you are no stowaway.

SYLVIA: No.

Pause.

EMMA: You have come here to tell me my papa is dead.

SYLVIA: No.

EMMA: Then... [*Beat.*] Oh. You are telling me I am dead.

SYLVIA: No—

EMMA: This is funny. I did always think of him, Papa, and if he is alive, or if he is not. But [*Laughing*] I never thought of this—that maybe I am the one dying, alone, on a boat. Alone, with a ghost.

SYLVIA: You're not dead. And I'm not a ghost.

EMMA: My mama, she *is* dead. And she told me once about the place in the woods, where all the men of one family go to die. Do you know this place too?

> *Pause.* SYLVIA *nods.*

You have been there?

SYLVIA: Yes.

EMMA: Wow…

> But you are really not here for me?

SYLVIA: No.

EMMA: Or my papa?

SYLVIA: I don't know him.

EMMA: That is good. That is good you do not know him. I think you are like me—I think we are good people not to know.

SYLVIA: Maybe. [*Pause.*] I have to say to you… I'm here to say—sail closer to the land tonight.

EMMA: I have not been to the land for many years.

SYLVIA: Not all the way, just… closer. Sail closer. And keep your eyes open.

EMMA: You would like me to?

SYLVIA: Yes.

> *Beat.*

EMMA: Then I will.

SYLVIA: Good.

EMMA: Good.

> *They watch one another.* EMMA *offers her a cigarette. She declines. A moment.*

SCENE TWENTY-SEVEN

NOAH *sits in the passenger seat.* ELISE *drives.*

NOAH: I woke up, on the bridge and… she was gone. I knew where she'd gone. I knew the water was beneath us and… I know it all but… But I don't know it. Because… it was never proven to me—because they could never show her to me—so I don't know it… I don't know.

Silence. He composes himself, laughs.

But—I do know she was Italian! And I do know I've never been there, to where she came from. And I've got this idiot friend who kept telling me I should do something.

CALEB *is seen in his drowning nightmare, and also in his reality.*

CALEB: Help! Help! Help me!

NOAH: And as is usually the way when idiots talk to you for long enough, eventually you listen to them. So here I am—hitching. I thought: If I can't say goodbye to her in England, why not say it, in the place she was before me?

Silence.

I'm so sorry. That was… so much talking. I don't usually… Sorry.

ELISE: Is okay. [*Beat.*] I think… I think you are so sad, Noah. I think you are really… (*wie sagt es?*) *filled up* with sadness, from this Italian wife you have lost. But I think lost is totally the wrong word. I think you carry her with you very much.

NOAH: Mm. Yeah, I do.

Have you lost anyone you love?

ELISE: No. I have found someone I love.

NOAH: Oh. That's good.

ELISE: No, is not. There is already another man I love, a husband I love. And now I have found one more.

NOAH: Oh.

ELISE: He has long hair and a belly. His name is Georg.

NOAH: Like George.

ELISE: *Ja.* Is very complicated.

She pulls over the car.

Here we are in Braunschweig. Here I leave you for the next driver.

Silence. Neither moves.

NOAH: Will you leave your husband?

ELISE: I am not sure. I love him. Will you leave your wife?

Beat.

NOAH: I'm not sure either.

Beat. She kisses him. They stop.

What was that?

ELISE: I... don't know honestly. Tonight I have argued with my husband. Tonight I am driving away from him. I was driving to the other man—but I cannot go there either. I do not want to be there now, or at home now. I need... I need this third place. Is okay with you?

NOAH: I feel guilty.

ELISE: But you do not know him.

NOAH: With Sophia. I feel guilty.

ELISE: Mm. I think... that is not how she works, Noah. I think... your wife went through your car window, as you said. And then you did not see her because... you could not see. Your head was hit. You were... unconscious.

But I think, she fell. And I think, she went into the water. And I think, when she hit the water... your wife would have died. And then she stopped being your wife. And then also she stopped being guilty.

This is what I imagine happened, and I feel very sad for you that it did.

Silence.

NOAH: I should go.

ELISE: Of course. But... then I am still in between.

She takes off her top.

ELISE: Then I am still needing somebody.

Beat.

NOAH: Your son.

ELISE: No, Jacob has heard everything. He knows everything.
He knows why I am doing this.

A held moment. They climb onto one another.

SCENE TWENTY-EIGHT

EMMA *watches an unconscious* CALEB, *concerned.*

EMMA: I am about the worst person you should meet if you are drowning in the sea. If it did not already have plans to kill you, then meeting me helps it to decide. You look like a very long and thin seal, with whiskers like it also. But your face looks not like a seal, but like a fish, the way nearly dead men's faces do. Your cheeks are sunk and your eyeballs stick out from your head.

> *Silence.* CALEB *splutters and comes to life.* EMMA *hits him hard to release the water, then takes his wetsuit off while he weakly protests.*

CALEB: Stop... I'm not wearing pants.

EMMA: I can see this. I can see your penis. I have a towel for you—here. Why are you in the middle of the ocean?

CALEB: I was swimming to Innisfail.

EMMA: Mm. You are near, I think. You nearly reached it.

CALEB: Yes.

EMMA: But then you nearly died.

CALEB: Yes.

EMMA: So it actually makes no difference if you have come near. Being dead and close is the same as being dead and far away.

> *Beat.*

CALEB: Yes. Are you... Why are you staring at me?

EMMA: You are alive. I have not seen someone alive for many years.

> *Silence.*

Because everyone I come near is then soon after dead.

> *Silence.*

Death. It is a really strange thing.

> CALEB *suddenly grabs the jag nearby.*

CALEB: Stay away from me!

EMMA: This was the jag that killed my brother Ulli. He didn't say very much for almost all his life. And then it went through beside his heart. And then his heart exploded against it. Honestly. Why are you holding it at me?

CALEB: You're trying to kill me.

EMMA: No, mister. Fate is maybe trying to kill you, and the sea too maybe. Or yourself—maybe you are stupid. But I am not a killer. I am just there when it happens. Anyway, why would I save you if to kill you later?

CALEB: I... I don't know. I don't know what's going on!

EMMA: You were nearly dead. If I had sailed a minute earlier or a minute later, or a mile left or a mile right, then yes, you are dead. That is the end. Goodnight mister. Enjoy the sea. My Mama is there.

CALEB: What—

EMMA: But I did sail just this way. And I was not practising my guitar (I am very good) or eating dinner or doing a shit. I was looking at the water. And hello, here is you in it. I did not have to be doing this. We did not have to meet. But we have. And because of this you are alive, instead of not. If this was me, I would be saying thank you maybe, and not wishing to stab someone with the jag that killed their brother. But that is me.

Silence. He puts the jag down.

CALEB: Sorry... I don't understand what's happening.

EMMA: No—you seem very confused. I think you have hypothermia. I think you will pass out soon.

CALEB: Can you... Please take me to a hospital.

EMMA: Mm. I have not found a port for years and years, so my Papa will survive. If I bring you to help, then I am bringing him maybe to death.

CALEB: Please... just...

He collapses, unconscious. She watches him and then wraps the towel around him.

EMMA: Do you really want my Papa to die, mister, so that you can live? Is that not too much for you to bear? Because I do not want to do something for you now, when you cannot argue, that will make you feel awful later.

But... it is nice you are alive, and I would like to keep you this way.

She watches him.

This is me thinking.

SCENE TWENTY-NINE

NOAH *and* ELISE *lie on neighbouring car seats, staring at the ceiling in silence. Eventually,* NOAH *turns to* ELISE *on his left and can only laugh, exasperated. He stares at her a long time, then returns his gaze to the ceiling.*

SCENE THIRTY

SYLVIA: They pull in very late, when it is very dark.

EMMA: I am thinking there is no one here and I must carry him—I am very strong. But—and this is a strange thing—there is someone there, a lady. And she is waiting. I have told nobody we are coming but she is waiting. And as I pull closer, I can see—she is the lady from the boat.

SYLVIA: The woman I met steers her boat in and without a word she throws me the rope. I loop it to a rail and when she draws close enough, we shake hands.

You've been at sea a long time.

EMMA: Many years.

SYLVIA: Without seeing anyone.

EMMA: Only you—the appearer and disappearer.

SYLVIA: Yes.

EMMA: Is this one with you?

CALEB: Sylvia Wist.

SYLVIA: Caleb Prosser. You nearly died.

CALEB: I'm not a strong enough swimmer. But I wanted to reach you. I know I can't surprise you—I know I'll never be able to surprise you. But I wanted to… do something surprising. Even if you knew about it already.

SYLVIA *helps him off the boat and looks at him.*

SYLVIA: I'm surprised.

EMMA *stares at the jetty for a long time and then determinedly climbs off the boat.*

EMMA: I need… We are in Innisfail, Australia.

SYLVIA: Yes.

EMMA: I need one Innisfail, Australia telephone.

SYLVIA *hands the mobile over.*

SYLVIA: Here.

EMMA: There are no buttons. I do not know what to do with—

SYLVIA: Press on the screen. You need 0011 first, and then a code.

EMMA: I know this code. Iceland has 354. And then... [*She enters the digits.*] ...Papa's number... and 2, and 4, and 4... And now do I press this—

SYLVIA: It will start rin—

EMMA: It is ringing. 'Scuse me.

EMMA *moves away and listens intently to the ringing.*

It becomes louder and louder. Slowly, the rings slow down and space out further and further, so that time seems stretched as she waits for the phone to connect.

ELISE: The Icelandic woman holds the phone very tightly, and listens to every ring very closely. And counts every ring very closely. The space in between becomes very... stretched. The woman who has stopped stares at the horizon.

NOAH: The man who has drowned stares at a woman.

EMMA: And the woman who is magic stares at a man.

CALEB: The man climbs from the car, zips up his jacket, and stares at the sleeping, German city that stretches before him.

SYLVIA: The woman with the child drives home, and puts the child to bed and walks quietly through the house. She enters a dark room where a man sleeps. She climbs gently into bed. She is unsure whether to lie on her left or her right. So she lies on her back.

So she stares at the ceiling.

Silence.

THE END

Brett Walsh as Noah and Christiaan Westerveld as Caleb in the 2012 Jute Theatre production in Cairns. (Photo: Romy Photography)

www.ingramcontent.com/pod-product-compliance
Lightning Source LLC
Chambersburg PA
CBHW041934090426
42744CB00017B/2049